Reference only

NORTHAMPTONSHIRE LIFE 1914–39

1. Relaxing in Wicksteed Park, Kettering, in the early Twenties.

NORTHAMPTONSHIRE LIFE 1914–39

A photographic survey

Compiled and Edited
by
R. L. GREENALL

Northamptonshire Libraries
1984

Published by
NORTHAMPTONSHIRE LIBRARIES
27 Guildhall Road, Northampton NN1 1EF

First published 1979
Reprinted 1984

Designed by Bernard Crossland Associates
Type set in Monotype Bembo 270, 11/12 pt.
and printed in Great Britain at
the Alden Press, Oxford

ACKNOWLEDGMENTS

The compiler wishes to thank the following owners and custodians of collections for granting permission to publish their photographs: Mr. J. W. Anscomb of Woodford Halse (30, 73, 74, 79, 82, 153, 172, 191): The Anglian Regimental Museum (Abington Park Museum) (8); Mrs. J. Brassington of Lowick (71, 136, 137, 147, 154, 192); Miss W. Breitmeyer, Great Addington Manor (20, 207, 208, 209); Canon P. J. M. Bryan of King's Cliffe (140); Mr. Alan Burman of Northampton (1, 3, 5, 18, 58, 69, 122, 163); Mr. Harold Clifton of Long Buckby (126, 162, 221); Daventry Charter Trustees (180); Mr. W. E. Elston (80, 119); Mr. Eric Fowell of Rushden (29, 36, 37, 38, 60, 68, 109); Mr. R. G. Foulkes of Nether Heyford (200); Mr. George Freeston of Blisworth (28, 40, 111, 133, 139, 197); *Flight International* (235, 236); Mr. M. J. Gibson of Higham Ferrers (124, 125, 127, 130); Mr. P. Hayward, Largs, Ayrshire (11); Mr. Roland Holloway of Northampton (177, 200, 201, 203, 211, 215, 222, 231, 233, 237, 238, 239); Mrs. Isobel Holmes of Northampton (219); The Imperial War Museum (13, 14); Mr. F. A. Moore of Kettering (9, 15, 43, 50, 57, 66, 67); Mr. G. Moore of Daventry (39, 169); Northampton Labour Party (224, 229, 230); Northampton Museums (31, 53, 54, 61, 62, 63, 64, 65, 97, 98, 102, 175); Northamptonshire Libraries (*tailpiece to Introduction*, 2, 17, 27, 35, 47, 49, 52, 83, 86, 88, 89, 90, 96, 99, 112, 113, 117, 149, 171, 195, 199, 204, 212, 213, 214, 218, 220, 223); Northamptonshire Record Office (16, 21, 22, 26, 46, 56, 59, 70, 100, 101, 102, 110, 121, 132, 143, 148, 151, 155, 156, 157, 164, 182–7, 194, 196, 198, 206, 216, 227, 234); Mr. J. J. A. Osborne of Higham Ferrers (48, 168, 174); Mr. and Mrs. M. Palmer of Earls Barton (25, 55, 84, 87, 115, 120); Mr. Cyril Putt of Raunds (32, 34, 41, 72, 105, 106, 116, 118, 135, 158, 165, 173, 178); Mr. F. Rabbitt of Wellingborough (179); Radio Times Hulton Picture Library (128, 129, 188); Mr. Colin Robinson of Whiston (4, 91, 92, 93, 94, 176); The Press Association Ltd. (217); Mr. Frank T. Thompson of Kettering (6, 10, 12, 19, 23, 24, 42, 44, 45, 75, 76, 77, 81, 85, 95, 104, 107, 108, 114, 123, 131, 138, 141, 142, 144–6, 150, 152, 160, 161, 166, 167, 181, 189, 190, 193, 202, 210, 225, 226, 228, 232); Mr. J. H. Thornton of Northampton (170); Mr. D. W. Turner of Braunston (78); Mr. Eric Westaway of Naseby (34, 51, 134, 159); and to the Northampton Mercury Company and the *Northamptonshire Evening Telegraph* for permission to reproduce photographs whose copyright they own. The compiler also would like to thank those who in any way helped with this publication, in particular Major D. Baxter, the Anglian Regiment, Northampton; Mr. P. I. King and his colleagues at the Northamptonshire Record Office; Mr. S. W. Nichols, Miss M. Arnold and other staff at Northampton Reference Library; Mr. W. N. Terry, Curator, and Miss J. M. Swann and Miss J. Hodgkinson of Northampton Museums; Mr. J. A. Munro, Deputy County Leisure and Libraries Officer and General Editor of the Libraries' publications; and Beedle and Cooper (Northampton) and R. Fielding for photographic work.

CONTENTS

INTRODUCTION

The purpose of this collection of photographs is not only to recapture the feel of life in Northamptonshire in the years 1914 to 1939 but also wherever possible to relate it to the broader pattern of national events so that the book has historical coherence, and is not merely 'a trip down Memory Lane'. The changes wrought in the fabric of English society by the events of these years were enormous, and their results by no means dead and academic. The Great War bled this country of its men and its wealth; it toppled Britain from its position of supremacy in the world; it began the disintegration of the Empire and the decline of the great industries of the nineteenth century. Its consequences included (amongst others) the emancipation of women; the rise of organized Labour; the collapse of Liberalism; the decline of the aristocracy; the rise of the modern mass media and the motor car; and 'the era of the common man'.

Modern Northamptonshire has recently been described as 'a county grappling with problems of rapid growth'.* By contrast, the years 1914 to 1939 saw scarcely any growth at all, as population statistics demonstrate quite clearly. In 1911 Northamptonshire's population was 304,000: by 1939 this had increased to 319,000, a growth of only 4·9 per cent. The reason for this lay not only with the prolonged decline of agriculture and changes in the size of families but more importantly with the stage reached in the evolution of shoemaking, the principal industry of Northamptonshire. Even before the Great War this trade had reached (and passed) its peak as an employer of labour, and steadily contracted in the Inter-War years. It was not, of course, then in decline; its output continued to rise, and it remained throughout our period the reliable staple trade of the county. The problem rather was that no other considerable industries came along to diversify the economy of the area. The result was that Northamptonshire preserved its late nineteenth-century character – that of a largely rural area with only one big town, Northampton (which was not all that populous),

* The Guardian 25 September 1974.

and pockets of industry in certain other towns and villages – well into the middle decades of the twentieth century. It was not until the Second World War that industrial diversification and population growth started to happen. In the Inter-War years, however, there was one exception to the pattern just outlined – the development of Corby. In the Twenties it was still a village, although the area around it had been quarried for iron ore since the 1880s, and a small ironworks had been developed from 1910. In the early Thirties, Stewarts and Lloyds, a Scottish firm, bought up a number of small iron and ironstone companies and made the decision to locate their steel tube plant close to the iron ore beds of Corby. No. 1 Blast Furnace to turn out 'Basic Bessemer' quality steel was lit in 1934. Corby was rapidly expanded, and by 1939 had grown from a village of 1,500 into a 'Garden City' of 10,000, many of the people migrating from Scotland.

Yet if Northamptonshire was marking time in economic matters, history was not passing it by. It experienced the great shake-up society was given by the Great War, as did other parts of Britain. In 1914 Northampton had soldiers of the Welsh Division billeted in the town. The Scottish Horse descended on a bedazzled Kettering. The ancient trades of the County – horse-dealing and boot and shoemaking – flourished as never before. Belgian refugees arrived. All age-groups and both sexes volunteered to 'do their bit'. In the opportunities it presented to women the war did more for their emancipation than all the efforts of the pre-war Suffrage movement. The war was a People's War, and civilians found themselves swept up in the multitude of activities involved in furthering the national effort. This period was the golden age of Volunteering, and, to the amazement of the rest of Europe, great armies were raised in Britain without conscription. But in 1916 with the sheer scale of the war, and the size of the casualty lists, came compulsion. The euphoria of late 1914 died in the terrible battles in France and Belgium, and Northamptonshire suffered its share of casualties at Mons,

Ypres, Loos, Neuve Chapelle, the Somme, Trônes Wood and Thiepval.

Finally the Great War ended with the Armistice of 11 November 1918 with people in a vengeful mood: Germany must be made to pay, the Kaiser and 'Little Willie' were (it was hoped) to stand trial for war crimes. The soldiers were demobilized and, somehow, in the year between the end of the war and Armistice Day 1919, the mood changed. Military pride changed into a deep-felt desire to salute the dead by raising memorials to them. Soon every town and village had one. They were, in effect, an emotional closing of the book on the Great War.

The politicians promised 'a land fit for heroes', but, after a short post-war boom, depression set in and most trades felt the pinch of unemployment, or, at best, of short-time. These years saw the rise of organized Labour, and a series of strikes, culminating in the General Strike of 1926. The shoe workers, however, were not militant: their battles had been fought in the 1890s, and well-established arbitration procedures had been laid down. The transport workers were, and there were strikes in Northamptonshire in 1915 and 1919. The General Strike of 1926, however, passed without much excitement locally. In these years Northamptonshire lay somewhere between the despairing mass-unemployment of the industrial coalfields and the prosperity of the centres of the new motor car and electrical industries in the Midlands and South-East. After the short-term changes of the Great War life returned to normal in the staple industries of this County.

Town life and rural life underwent no great changes. Modernization there was: streets were widened; new banks were opened on the prime corner sites; some slums were demolished; new fire and police stations were built. Housing estates of 'semis' were laid out, and the first 'Council houses' were built and occupied. Compared to forty years previously the countryside had emptied of its people. Rural labourers, once so numerous, continued to migrate to the towns. Mechanization on the farm, however, was surprisingly slow in coming. The rural way of life was modified, but not seriously undermined, in these years. Squalid village cottages were demolished and Council estates made their first appearance; but the middle-class urban commuter had not yet moved into the village in force. Yet personal mobility, that transformer of modern society, was just around the corner. The motor car was a pre-war invention, but the war accelerated its technology, as it did the aircraft's. Ownership of both kinds of machine widened after 1918, though the middle-classes monopolized them. The internal combustion engine killed the electric trams and hastened the decline of the railways. Buses and private cars improved rural communications, and parochialism began to decline. Sywell airport opened in 1928 and for a decade the middle and upper-classes indulged in the sport of 'Flying for Fun'. The great figures of the day – among them airborne women such as Amy Johnson and the elderly Duchess of Bedford – touched down on the airfield in their Tiger Moths.

In the Twenties leisure was also transformed by the spread of the internal combustion engine. This was the golden age of the 'outing': trips by chara-banc were cleaner and less constrained by time-tables than in the days of the railway excursion. In any case social attitudes were more relaxed generally. The young were more uninhibited than their parents and grandparents; dancing was more outrageous in the 'jazz era'; concert parties flourished, as did fêtes, carnivals and hospital parades. All these were essentially community enjoyments. The cinema became enormously popular, and by 1939 virtually every home had a wireless: by then people were increasingly taking their entertainment more individually and passively. In 1925 the sleepy Northamptonshire town of Daventry became a household word ('Daventry calling') when the BBC erected its first high-power transmitter ('5XX') on Borough Hill.

Yet despite all the changes, tradition remained strong in leisure and pleasure as in other social matters. If the working-class took a continuing pleasure in football and cricket, the well-to-do clung vigorously to the pleasures associated with horse and hound. The aristocracy and the gentry found the life-style of the Edwardian era was no longer possible: it had become too expensive and the pool of domestic servants had largely evaporated. Some estates under the pressures of personal extravagance, new taxation and the depression in agriculture had been broken up – the Duke of Grafton sold out in 1919–20, and the Knightleys in the Thirties. Yet, despite this, and the loss of political power, the landed-classes were still deferred to. Moreover, Northamptonshire was an attractive rural area, not too far from London and new monied people moved in and assumed the role of gentry. A new concept of social leadership-through-public-service came in to replace leadership-through-the-magistracy. Some squires' sons and daughters made names in professions not hitherto associated with the landed-classes – music, drama and scholarship. Royal visits were made to the county on 'official' business at regular intervals, and the Jubilee of King George V and his Queen was celebrated in 1935 and the Coronation of George VI and Queen Elizabeth in 1937. The Duke of York (later George VI) took a house for the hunting season for several years in the Twenties, and the Duke of Gloucester settled at Barnwell after his marriage.

This period saw considerable political changes. The rural constituencies remained traditionally Conservative, but after two Coalitions under the premiership of Lloyd George in the years 1916 to 1922, the Liberal party, once so strong in North-hampton, Kettering and Wellingborough, disintegrated. Here, as elsewhere in Britain, politics polarized around class with the rise of the Labour Party to importance in the once-Liberal towns.

The approach of war in the years 1938–9 found Northamptonshire unprepared, as it did the rest of the country. After the war memorials had been erected following the Great War, the British were only too glad to forget about war, except on one day a year. Rearmament was politically unpopular in the Twenties and Thirties; English life had remained fundamentally unchanged despite the Great War; and the implications of the rise of Fascism were carefully ignored until almost too late. Our period ends with the alarming realization that England was woefully unprepared for a new holocaust.

February 1984   R.L.GREENALL

A May Day garland at Braybrooke, 1919.

THE GREAT WAR

2. Soldiers of the Northamptonshire Regiment leave Kettering on 6 August 1914 to join the British Expeditionary Force in Belgium. *Evans, Kettering.*

**Gott en Hemmel!—
Here kom der NORTHAMPTONS
from SHEERNESS.**

3. Regulars of the Royal Welch Fusiliers training at Higham Ferrers in 1914.

4. The mood of August 1914: patriotic, euphoric, simple-minded.

5. War fever. 'The East Street Bantam Fusiliers', local children of East Street and district, Wellingborough Road, Northampton, drilling.

6. The Regulars depart: the Scottish Horse, having used Kettering as a Remount Depot, about to leave for the Front in 1915. In the boater is Councillor Gravestock, Chairman of the Urban District Council. *Spencer Percival.*

7. The Royal Welch Fusiliers, after training in Northampton, about to leave for the Front, October 1914.

8. Volunteering: the rugby player as hero. An international in the years 1909–10, Edgar Mobbs was Northampton's most famous rugby player. Rejected at the outbreak of war as 'too old' (he was 32) he set out to form a company from amongst his sporting friends when the age limit was raised for Kitchener's army. The response was amazing. Within a very short space of time some 400 men had contacted him of whom 264 passed the medical test. They became part of the 7th Battalion of the Northamptonshire Regiment, and fought throughout the war on the Western Front. Starting as a private, by 1917 Mobbs had won the DSO and was Lieutenant-Colonel commanding the 7th Battalion. He was killed in action in the Ypres Salient on 31 July that year. He was seen as the very epitome of the volunteer-patriot and is perhaps unique in having a personal monument in his home town. His name is also kept alive to this day by the annual Mobbs Memorial rugby match. In the photograph he is seen with a shrapnel wound sustained in 1916.

9. Volunteering: Kettering men joining up in the Scottish Horse. *Spencer Percival.*

10. New recruits being introduced to the niceties of puttee drill at Kettering. *Spencer Percival.*

11. Life at the Front: concert party of the 7th Northamptons in 1917. Seated in the centre is Lieutenant-Colonel Mobbs.

12. Officers of the 4th Battalion, the Northamptonshire Regiment in 1920. In the centre (with walking stick) is Lieutenant-Colonel John Brown, the Commanding Officer. A Northampton man who joined the Volunteers at the time of the Boer War, he served with the Battalion right through the Gallipoli campaign and in Egypt and Palestine. In 1918 he was awarded the DSO, and in 1920, when the 4th Northamptons were re-formed as a territorial battalion, he was appointed officer commanding. He was knighted in 1934.

13. Behind the lines at the Front. The 1st Northamptons parade before the Duke of Connaught near Bruay, July 1918.

14. Behind the lines. Men of the 7th Battalion in camp at Dickebusch, August 1917.

15. Belgian refugees at Kettering, October 1914. In the light suit and cap (centre) is William Ballard, Secretary of the Kettering Industrial Co-operative Society.

16. Belgian officers and their families at the Manor House, Brackley in November 1914. Seated centre is Miss Beatrice Cartwright.

17. Carnival and parade in aid of Belgian refugees at Thrapston in 1914.

18. Northamptonshire's 'concentration camp' at Eastcote House. In 1914 Germans living in the area were interned. They ranged from the Modern Languages master at Rugby school to shopkeepers and manual workers. To while away the time they made this model of the Dardanelles.

Kettering St John Voluntary Aid Detachment.

19. One way women could play a significant part in the war effort was by volunteering to become VADs, and work in the hastily expanded hospital services. *Spencer Percival*.

20. Wounded soldiers at Rushton Hall in 1914. The owners of many country houses opened them as temporary hospitals or convalescent homes at the start of the war.

21. A team competing at the Red Cross Fête at Aynho, June 1916.

22. The winning team from Towcester. The boy scout acted as wounded soldier or accident victim.

23. Wounded soldiers recovering at the Kettering VAD hospital in 1915. Note their cap badges, showing that they came from many different regiments, including one ANZAC soldier. *Spencer Percival.*

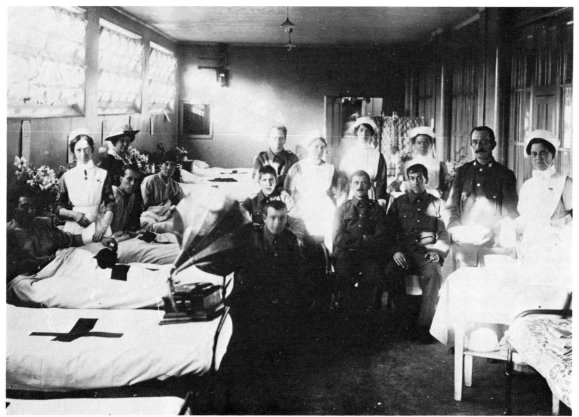

24. A ward in the Kettering VAD hospital in July 1915. *Spencer Percival.*

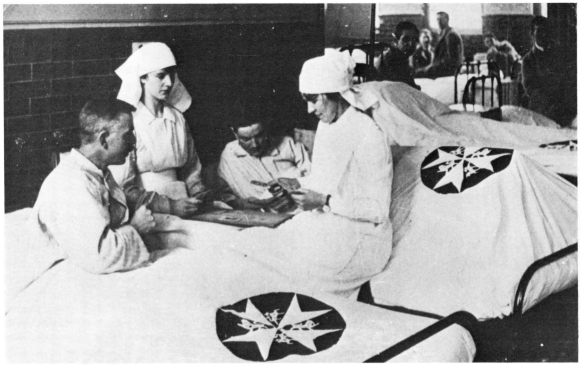

25. Wellingborough VAD hospital in late 1918. Some thirty quilts had been decorated with the emblem of the Order of St. John of Jerusalem by Mrs. Owen (right) seen playing cards with Sister Cook and two patients.

Ward 5. War Hospital.

26. A ward in the War Hospital, Duston, Northampton, now St. Crispin Hospital.

27. Soldiers and members of the Women's Land Army baling straw for bedding, Home Farm, Potterspury, about 1916.

28. Members of the Women's Land Army at work on a farm in the Brackley area in 1917.

29. Women doing men's jobs in the footwear industry at Rushden. For the first time ever women were allowed to work in the 'Rough Stuff' room at the Co-operative Wholesale Society factory in 1917. Hitherto their work has been confined to closing.

30. Women cleaners employed at the railway sheds at Woodford Halse, about 1917.

31. Surgeon-Lieutenant H. F. Percival of Northampton. He served on HMS *Tiger* and *Africa* and was at the battle of Jutland. *Swaine, New Bond Street and Southsea.*

32. A regular, Corporal William Stringer of Raunds. He won the Military Medal in 1916. He was killed in action in 1917. *C. W. Vorley.*

33. Corporal Harry Westaway of Prince Rupert's Farm, Sibbertoft in 1914. He was killed in November 1917. His name is on the Naseby War Memorial, *see 51.*

34. Two Raunds men in the Royal Horse Artillery home on leave before leaving for the Front; T. Rollings (left) and William Brawn (right). *C. W. Vorley.*

35. Sergeant Robert Sear of Northampton of the Royal Flying Corps. He was reported killed over German lines while on a raid, 26 September 1918.

36. Sergeant William Ewart Boulter, VC, 6th Battalion the Northamptonshire Regiment, at Rushden. He is seen with Mr. Tysoe, manager of the CWS shoe factory on the occasion of his visit in 1916 to boost morale. He had won his VC on the 14th July at Trônes Wood on the Western Front.

34

35

36

37. The loss of life in the battles of 1916 and 1917 began to bring home to civilians the reality of the war. When the boy next door was killed casualties ceased to be just names in the local paper. A desire to commemorate the dead first took the form of street shrines, the first of which apparently appeared in Rushden, like this one in the High Street. Other towns soon followed suit.

38. The Rev. Charles Keeler, Methodist minister, gives an address at a 'war shrine' in Rushden in 1917.

39. The 'war shrine' in the Market Place, Daventry. The girl is Miss Hammond, the schoolmaster's daughter.

40. A war wedding in 1916 between Lieutenant Harold Cookson, the Worcestershire Regiment, and Sarah Griffith, a Blisworth farmer's daughter. After the war the couple lived at Birmingham.

41. The wedding photograph of Mr. and Mrs. Walter Putt of Raunds in 1916. Mr. Putt served with the Northamptons and the Machine Gun Corps and survived the war.

42. Civilian fund raising. The Duchess of Buccleuch opens a Farmers' Great Jumble Auction at Kettering, 11 June 1915. On her left is Councillor Gravestock, Chairman of the Urban District Council. *Spencer Percival*.

43. One of the results of civilian fund raising: Kettering's first field ambulance, 1917.

44. A captured German gun presented by the Government to the postmaster of Aldwincle. Although his village had only 300 people Mr. J. W. Julyan sold £18,400 worth of war savings certificates. *Spencer Percival.*

45. The Army's way of saying 'Thank you' at the end of the war. As a reward for raising about £2 million in war savings, Kettering was presented with a tank. It was a 'female' (said to be more vicious than the 'male') and weighed 28 tons. Here it is seen leaving Kettering railway station.

46. Captioned 'What happened to the Kaiser and Little Willie at Brackley, November 11 1918', this picture catches the vengeful mood of the nation at the end of the war. The Kaiser was not, in the event, tried as a war criminal, but the sentiment of 'making Germany pay' was reflected in the Treaty of Versailles, with disastrous results for Europe.

This Shield was Presented
BY
Councillor HENRY BUTTERFIELD, J.P.
to the Infants of Campbell Square School
in recognition of their Services to
Wounded Soldiers during the last year
of the Great War - having collected the
largest per-centage of Eggs per Scholar
of any similar Department in
the Elementary Schools of
the Borough of Northampton.
1919

47. A reward for junior war work.

NOT
FORGETTING

48. The unveiling of the war memorial at Higham Ferrers,
Armistice Day 1921.

49. The march-past at the temporary wooden cenotaph outside Kettering Library, 11 November 1919. At first it was intended to commemorate the first anniversary of the ending of the war by victory marches of service men. But by November 1919 the mood had changed from one of militarism to that of a powerful desire to salute dead comrades. So the idea of a cenotaph, an empty tomb, as the symbol of the fallen, came into being. At first the cenotaphs were temporary and made of wood, like this one.

50. The permanent Memorial to the fallen at Kettering, unveiled in 1921.

51. The war memorial at Naseby, erected March 1921. The choice of a rather tired lion, though unusual, was not inappropriate.

52. The unveiling of the war memorial at Pitsford.

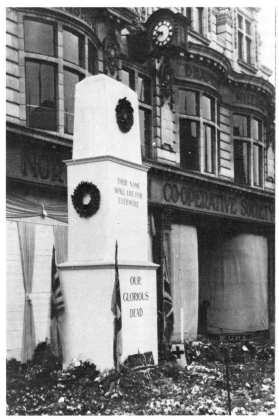

53. The temporary wooden cenotaph in Abington Street, Northampton, in 1919.

55. The Prince of Wales laying a wreath at the cenotaph in Northampton, 7 July 1927. Designed by Lutyens, the memorial had been unveiled the previous year.

54. The memorial to Lieutenant-Colonel Edgar Mobbs in its original location in the Market Place at Northampton. It was unveiled by Lord Lilford in July 1921. The figure on top is the Goddess of Fame.

56. Unveiling the war memorial at Walgrave, February 1921.

57. The Armistice Day march-past of Ex-servicemen in Kettering about 1925. The two minutes silence at 11 a.m. on the 11th November each year was observed religiously across the nation in this period, and was a ritual charged with the deepest emotion. It was accompanied by an Ex-servicemen's march to the local war memorial for wreath-laying ceremonies.

58. The opening of the Garden of Remembrance in Abington Square, Northampton in 1937. A wall recording the names of the men from the town who lost their lives in the war, and the Mobbs monument, moved from the Market Place, are its focal points.

59. A humbler memorial to the men of Clipston who fell in the war, in the parish church.
Lumbers, Leicester.

INDUSTRIAL
LIFE

60. Shoe workers at the CWS factory in Rushden in
the Great War. Note the hair style of the period.

61. Factory life: the closing room at the Mounts
Factory in Northampton, 1919. *H. Cooper and Son.*

62. The closing room at Lowke Bros., Kettering, 1929.

63. 'Handsewn men' at Charles Smith Ltd., Henry Street, Northampton in 1939.

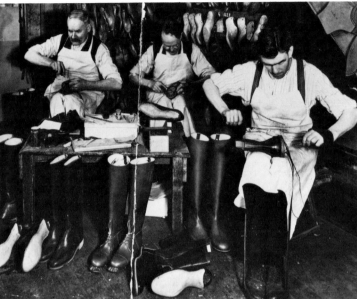

64. A new footwear factory of the period: Timpson's, Bath Road, Kettering, built in 1922. The firm closed it in 1972.

65. The Making Room,
Mounts Factory Company,
Northampton 1919.

66. The clothing industry. Work in the 'Ladies' Costumes' cutting room, Kettering Clothing Manufacturing Co-operative Society Ltd., in 1923.

67. The large machine room for 'Gentlemen's Fashions' at the same factory. It is said to have accommodated 800 employees.

68. The iron industry. Islip Furnaces, which closed down on 16 October 1942.

69. Corby works in 1936.

70. Workers of the Lloyd Ironstone Company in a quarry near Corby getting stone for 'Tarmac' roads in 1922. *Speight, Kettering.*

71. Quarrymen at Lowick, about 1930.
72. Gas workers at Raunds in the Twenties.

73. A locomotive under the 'Sheer Legs' at Woodford Locomotive works in the Twenties. This was a lifting device to raise the body of the engine off the wheels.

74. Workers in the Waggon Shop, Woodford Halse Works, in the early Twenties.

75. The rise of organized labour. Banner of the Amalgamated Society of Railway Servants displayed in the transport strike of 1919. Believed to have been taken at Wellingborough.

76. A trades union demonstration at Wellingborough in 1915.

77. A Railwaymen's demonstration in Kettering, believed to be in 1915. *Spencer Percival.*

78. A scene from a rather bitter boatmen's strike at Braunston in 1924. Notice the two lines of policemen presumably protecting 'blacklegs'.

79. The General Strike of 1926. The Woodford and Hinton strike committee. They were all railwaymen, members of either ASLEF or the NUR.

80. The General Strike. The contingent of Northampton policemen sent to Hucknall in Nottinghamshire, October to November 1926. Their task was to protect miners returning to work from interference by those staying out.

81. Footwear workers voting at Kettering Trades Club on whether or not to take a wage cut or strike in the early Thirties. The face of the official, J. E. Chapman (second from the left) is a study in the necessary boredom involved in much trade union work.

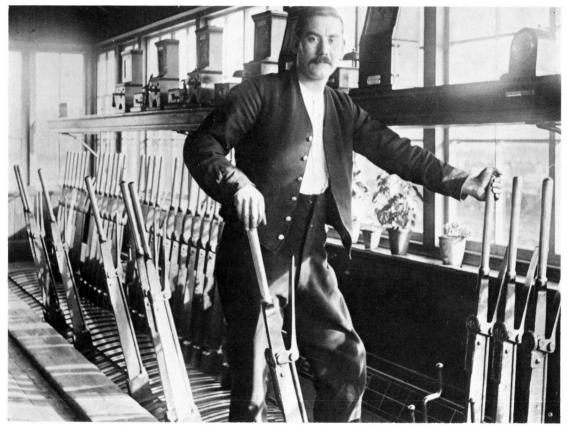
82. A. Gardner in his signal box at Woodford Halse, probably during the Great War.

TOWN LIFE

83. The corner of the Drapery and Mercers Row, before the building of the Westminster Bank in 1925.

84. The Christmas market, Wellingborough, 1914.

85. A familiar street scene in the Twenties: a mechanical organ with moving figures on top photographed in Victoria Street, Kettering. *Spencer Percival.*

86. Modernization: the demolition of an historic Northampton inn, the *George*, in 1921. The site had been bought by Lloyds Bank.

87. Modernization: taking part of the churchyard to widen Church Street, Wellingborough in 1932.

88. Part of old Northampton which still survives: Drum Lane, photographed in February 1914. All Saints Church forms the background. *C. F. Allen.*

89. Old Northampton: South Court, off Cattle Market Road. On the left is the Victorian mission church of St. Luke's, in the parish of All Saints. The church and court were demolished in 1930. Mulliner's Garage was later to occupy this site. In the background the Northampton Brewery Co. looms.

90. Modern Developments in the Thirties. The new police and fire stations on the site of the old Borough gaol, Upper Mounts, Northampton. Pevsner describes the architecture of the fire station as 'desperately uninspired'.

91. Modernism: a
bedroom at 78
Derngate, Northampton,
a terraced house
remodelled for W. J.
Bassett-Lowke in
1916–17 by Charles
Rennie Mackintosh of
the Glasgow School
of Art – 'the Father of
Modern Architecture'.

92. Bernard Shaw with
Mrs. Bassett-Lowke
outside the front door
of 78 Derngate in
1922. Shaw was in
Northampton to
support Margaret
Bondfield, the Labour
candidate for the
Borough.

93. The hall at 78 Derngate.

94. The lounge of 'New Ways' in 1926, a new house designed by Behrens for W. J. Bassett-Lowke. Note the illuminated 'windows', Mondrian style, on either side of the fireplace, the original posters on the walls, and the carpet 'Summer'.

95. 'Homes fit for heroes'. The first council tenants, Mr. James Hough and family, move into their house in the Windmill Avenue estate, Kettering, in 1921.

96. The eastern growth of Northampton in 1926: the Abington housing estate viewed from the north. Abington Park and the Wellingborough Road are at the top of the photograph. The houses are 'twelve per acre semi-detached'. *Aerofilms Ltd.*

97. A Northampton shop, Kendall's, 50 The Drapery, in the Twenties.

98. The same shop after modernization in 1935.

99. The new swimming baths, Upper Mounts, Northampton, opened October 1936. *Henry Cooper and Son*.

100. Housing for the workers in the new 'garden city' of Corby put up in the 1930s. *Lumbers, Leicester.*

101. The shopping centre at Corby, built in the late Thirties. *Lumbers, Leicester.*

103. James Manfield, photographed in the doorway of Weston Favell House before he gave it to the town. The second son of Sir Philip Manfield, the Victorian shoe manufacturer, he played an active role in the civic life of the town, being Mayor in 1902 and 1905. He died in 1925.

102. A plaque telling the story of a Northampton hospital.

MANFIELD
ORTHOPÆDIC HOSPITAL
NORTHAMPTON
FOUNDED · · · 1925
THIS TABLET IS ERECTED
IN GRATEFUL REMEMBRANCE OF
JAMES MANFIELD, ESQ, J.P.
WHO, IN 1924
GAVE HIS HOUSE AND GROUNDS TO
THE NORTHAMPTON & COUNTY
CRIPPLED CHILDREN'S FUND
AND AS A TRIBUTE TO ALL
WHO BY THEIR VOLUNTARY SERVICE
AND GENEROUS GIFTS DEVELOPED
AND SUPPORTED THIS HOSPITAL
FOR TWENTY THREE YEARS.

THE HOSPITAL WITH ITS ENDOWMENTS
WAS TAKEN INTO THE
NATIONAL HEALTH SERVICE
5TH JULY, 1948.

"FAC RECTE NIL TIME"

104. 'A mile of pennies' in Hospital Week in Burton Latimer, October 1922. Annual 'Hospital Weeks' with their pageants, processions and cycle parades were a familiar feature of life in the inter-war period.

105. Selling balloons for Hospital Day at Raunds in the early Twenties.
The sellers are Mrs. Abbott (left) and Mrs. Pettit.

HOSPITAL PARADE. RAUNDS.

106. The Hospital Day parade in the gateway of the Hall gardens at Raunds in the early Twenties.
C. W. Vorley.

107. Fighting a serious fire at Mobbs and Lewis, Kettering, in 1921.
Spencer Percival.

108. Rush hour in Kettering, about 1930. The location is the corner of
Rockingham Road and Dryden Street. The women are clothing workers from the
Co-operative factories in Dryden Street and Field Street.

TRANSPORT

109. The airship R101 over Higham Ferrers in 1930.
Shortly after it crashed spectacularly at Beauvais on its test flight to India.
E. Randell.

110. A sign of the railways in decline. Offord Bridge station on the Stamford to Wansford line, closed in 1929.

111. Narrow boat at the north portal of the Blisworth tunnel, Grand Junction Canal, 1921. *W. Alexander*.

112. Electric tram outside All Saints, Northampton, 1927. The trams were shortly to fall victims to the internal combustion engine.

113. Members of the Transport Committee of the Northampton Borough Council drive the last Northampton tram on its final journey, 15 December 1934.

114. Rural transport. Buses on the Cattle Market, Kettering, in the Twenties.

115. The first motor bus in Earls Barton, 1921. It was owned by Jack Wills, the village carrier.

116. The Wellingborough bus at Raunds, in the early Twenties.
C. W. Vorley.

117. A sign of the times. A Grose breakdown van with an accident victim in tow on the Market Place, Northampton, in the Twenties.

118. Heighton's Garage, Thrapston, about 1919. The firm are still there. The prices of the cars for sale range from £170 to £250. *C. W. Vorley.*

119. PC W. E. Elston in one of the first police cars in Northampton in 1935. They were BSA three-wheelers.

120. A six-ton 'under' type steam waggon built by the firm of Richard Garrett of Leiston, Suffolk, in September 1926.

121. The pleasure of country motoring: view of the Welland Valley viaduct. *Lumbers, Leicester.*

122. Country motoring: outside the gates of Lamport Hall, H. J. Leeson poses in his new 9-horse-power 4-cylinder Rover in 1924. This model cost £180 in that year. *H. J. Leeson.*

123. Miss E. M. Mansbridge, nurse of Thrapston and district, with the motor
scooter subscribed by the villages of her district in October 1923.
Delight is written all over her face. *Spencer Percival*.

124. Amy Johnson arrives at Sywell in 1934. In 1930 Miss Johnson (who liked to be known as 'Johnnie') had been the first woman to fly to Australia. In 1932 she flew solo to the Cape and in 1933 to Connecticut. She was killed in a flying accident in 1941.

125. Miss Johnson surrounded by juvenile admirers.

126. In 1929 these aircraft were at Long Buckby offering 'flips' at half-a-crown a time. The small boy is Tom Underwood.

127. More flying ladies. Miss Dorothy Spicer (centre) and Miss Pauline Gower (right) not only flew as a hobby, but ran an air taxi business from their own aerodrome at Hunstanton as well. They are seen at the first All-Women's Air Display at Sywell, September 1931. Miss Spicer was the first woman to qualify for all the Air Ministry's general licences for ground engineers, and Miss Gower was the first woman to hold the Air Ministry's 1st-class certificate for navigation.

128. Miss Tyzack with the bouquet she dropped from the aeroplane to the Duchess of Bedford (who herself took to flying in her sixties) at the first All-Women's Air Display at Sywell, 19 September 1931. *Radio Times Hulton Picture Library*.

129. The first All-Women's Air Display at Sywell, September 1931, organized by the Women's Committee of the Northamptonshire Aero Club. *Radio Times Hulton Picture Library*.

130. Newlyweds Mr. and Mrs. E. T. Danson of Rushden about to leave by aeroplane on their honeymoon in Paris in April 1934. The groom was a pilot member of the Northamptonshire Aero Club. There was a craze for 'aerial weddings' at that time.

131. Kettering: a weighing machine that could not take the weight of a steam waggon hauling a load of sand going to the construction of the new Timpson Shoe Factory in June 1922. *Spencer Percival.*

RURAL LIFE

132. Photograph of an agricultural worker entitled, simply,
'the mower'. *H. Cooper & Son.*

133. Three Blisworth women and others at work at Pell's Farm, Milton Malsor, during or soon after the Great War.

134. Farmer Goswick Westaway and his home-made hay sweep at Naseby, about 1932.

135. Farmer Thomas Warth and workers, the Grange, Raunds, about 1920. *C. W. Vorley.*

136. The annual timber sale on the Drayton estate in the Twenties.

137. Four forestry workers on the Drayton estate.

138. A get-together of gamekeepers of the Kettering district in the Twenties. *Spencer Percival.*

139. Haymaking, Royal Oak paddock, Blisworth, about 1918. *Walter Alexander.*

140. Gifts of rabbits after a shoot at King's Cliffe, about 1921.

141. A bailiff's eviction in the Twenties, place and person unknown.

142. Tips from the Trenches. Villagers at Geddington cooking on sawdust ovens, an old soldiers' ruse, during the fuel shortage of 1921.
Spencer Percival.

143. Rural charities: inmates of the Jesus Hospital at Rothwell entertained
to Christmas dinner in 1930 by Mr. Norman Butlin (seated), landlord of
the *Sun Inn*. This almshouse for poor men was founded in 1590 by Owen
Ragsdale who endowed it with his Manor of Old, and other lands. It still
exists, now providing accommodation for married couples.

144. Village Charities: the interest of £300 left by Sir Robert Dallington
in 1636 provided bread weekly, and money after service on Christmas
morning, for 24 poor people of Geddington. Here the rector and
churchwardens are seen distributing the money in 1924.
Spencer Percival.

146. An old Corby village custom: the letting of the 'church and town lands' at a 'pin and candle auction' in 1928. The two lots of grazing land (5 acres in all) were let to the person who made the last bid before the pin fell out of the tallow candle. Canny bidders would keep silent as long as possible and then try to get in a low bid just before the pin fell. The income raised this way was divided between the churchwardens and the trustees of the parish poor. The tenancy of the land was for four years and on this occasion went to a bid of £10 a year. *Spencer Percival.*

145. Surviving village customs. At Broughton the feast night in December was celebrated by a 'tin kettle parade' at the witching hour. In the early Thirties attempts were made in the magistrates' court to suppress this boisterous custom, without much success. The photograph was taken in 1928. *Spencer Percival.*

147. Lowick Church Choir about 1932. The rector was the Rev. A. S. Hazel.

148. The committee of the Brackley Women's Institute photographed on the 16th July 1924 at Aynho Park. The occasion was the coming of age of R. F. W. C. Cartwright, son of Sir Fairfax Cartwright. Miss Beatrice Cartwright, Mayor of the Borough in 1922–4 and 1934–6, is seated in the centre.

149. Friendly Societies: members of the Royal and Ancient Order of Buffaloes, Wellingborough Lodge, about 1920.

150. Friendly Societies: the rally of the Ancient Order of Foresters at Geddington Cross in August 1922. Giving the address is the Rev. Paul Bush, rector of Little Oakley. *Spencer Percival.*

151. The village at play: the 'Peace Day' carnival at Great Weldon, 1919.

152. The village at play: the opening of Rothwell Fair, June 1922. The Elizabethan Market House built by Sir Thomas Tresham is in the background.

153. A village band from Woodford Halse in the Twenties. It was known as the 'beer and bacca' band to differentiate it from the other band (presumably 'Temperance') in the village.

154. May Day celebrations at the village school, Lowick, in the late Thirties.

155. Wayfaring old style: a gypsy caravan crossing the bridge over the Nene at Fotheringhay in the late Thirties. *Lumbers, Leicester.*

156. Wayfaring new style: motorists pose at the foot of the steep street of Rockingham village in the early Thirties. *Lumbers, Leicester.*

157. A dead village: one of the last cottages at Faxton still standing in the Thirties.
Lumbers, Leicester.

158. An expanding village. The felling of Crow Spinney, Raunds, about 1920.

159. The May Day procession at Naseby, 1931. The May Queen was Mary Toseland.

160. A village fête. Lady Manningham-Buller (third from left) and Mrs. G. Ripley
(with sunshade) make purchases at Bury House, Cottingham, about 1921.
Spencer Percival.

LEISURE AND PLEASURE

161. A Wicksteed see-saw at Wicksteed Park, Kettering, about 1921.
Spencer Percival.

162. The inter-war years were the golden age of scouting: Long Buckby scouts returning from camp at Canons Ashby in 1923.

163. The scout troop of Christ Church, Northampton, in the Twenties.

164. The Boys' Brigade Company, Duston, in 1922. Based on the Congregational Church (now United Reformed) the company is exceptionally vigorous to this day.

165. The Girl Guide Company of Raunds Wesleyan Church, about 1932. *C. W. Vorley.*

166. Wicksteed Park, Kettering. In 1914 Charles Wicksteed, owner of an engineering works, bought 80 acres on the Barton Seagrave side of Kettering to make a park for the town. He spent in excess of £50,000 laying it out. Here from his motor car he watches the children at the pond for model boats. *Spencer Percival.*

167. Kettering people at Wicksteed Park in the early Twenties.

168. The outing to Cambridge of Horace Wright's Factory, Rushden, in 1920.
169. Daventry Town Bowling Club's outing to Builth Wells, 1922.

170. The jazz era. 'The Dixie Dance Band', an amateur group from Kettering. On the left is John H. Thornton, for many years the head of the Boot and Shoe Department at Northampton College of Technology (now part of Nene College). The others are Arthur Ansell (drums), Arthur Asher (violin), Arthur Gotch (saxophone), Arthur Knight (piano) and Pat Thornton (brother of John and a well-known Kettering jeweller) (saxophone).

171. Concert parties: 'The Jolly Girls', a group associated with the Methodist Church, Higham Ferrers, about 1920.

172. 'The Red and White Concert Party' from Woodford Halse in the Twenties. Their main efforts went to help the Liberal cause.

173. Ambrose Ferry and George Hall, two Raunds men, as 'Weary Willie' and 'Tired Tim' (two characters from 'Comic Cuts'). They were regulars in any carnival, procession or fête in the Raunds and Thrapston district in the years around 1930.
C. W. Vorley.

174. Employees of Sanders and Sanders as 'Dolls in a Box' ready for the Carnival Parade, Rushden, about 1937.

175. Northamptonshire men love their allotments, and since the early
nineteenth century have held annual horticultural shows. Here the display
of the Society at Manfield and Sons Ltd., Northampton is being judged,
about 1930.

176. The theatre: Tom Osborne Robinson (left), the youthful stage designer at the Repertory Theatre, Northampton, at work in 1928 with the producer, H. M. Prentice, on scenery for the Expressionist play 'RUR'. The play was futuristic (set in the 1950s) and about Mechanized Man.

177. 'On and Off Stage' at the New Theatre, Northampton, in the late Thirties. *Roland Holloway.*

178. The early years of the cinema. Sergeant Dunmore, the commissionaire at the Palace, Raunds, in the early Twenties. *C. W. Vorley.*

179. The staff and orchestra of the Corn Exchange Cinema (later the Regal), Wellingborough, about 1922. The orchestra, of course, eventually became redundant after 1927 when talking pictures came in.

180. The entry of radio: the official opening of the high-power transmitter (the BBC's first) at Daventry, 27 July 1925. It was performed by the Postmaster-General, Sir William Mitchell-Thomson, Bt. (holding paper). On his right is the Mayor of Daventry (Councillor I. H. Johnson) and behind them Mr. J. C. W. (later Lord) Reith, Managing Director of the BBC, gazes sternly at the camera.

181. Radio as a novelty: the first wireless-set in the Kettering Workhouse, 1925. *Spencer Percival.*

182. Sport: a shooting party on the Cartwright estate at Aynho, 6 September 1922.

183. The Pytchley Hunt leaving Brixworth, November 1934, led by Stanley Barker, the huntsman, followed by the Joint Masters, Lieutenant-Colonel J. G. Lowther and Captain R. Macdonald-Buchanan.

184. The Army Point-to-Point Steeplechase at Great Brington, March 1930.
Sport and General Press Agency Ltd.

185. (*From the left*). Lord and Lady Cromwell with Brigadier-General Little at the Pytchley Hunt
Point-to-Point meeting at Holdenby, March 1930. *Sport and General Press Agency Ltd.*

187. Mrs. Hewson (left) and Miss Blacklock at the Pytchley Point-to-Point in March 1930.
Sport and General Press Agency Ltd.

186. 'A fair spectator on a precarious perch' at the Army Point-to-Point steeplechase at Great Brington, 1930
Sport and General Press Agency Ltd.

188. Meet of the Grafton Foxhounds at Brackley, November 1931.
W. Pope, the huntsman, is seen taking the stirrup cup.
Radio Times Hulton Picture Library.

189. Lady Lowther at a race meeting in the Twenties.

190. Spectators and a member of the hunt, some time in the Twenties. Place and date uncertain. *Spencer Percival*.

191. The local champions: Woodford Central FC in 1921.
With one exception they were all railwaymen.

192. Lowick Tennis Club team, 1930. They won 627 games out of 900 in the Brigstock League and won the Bellville Cup that year.

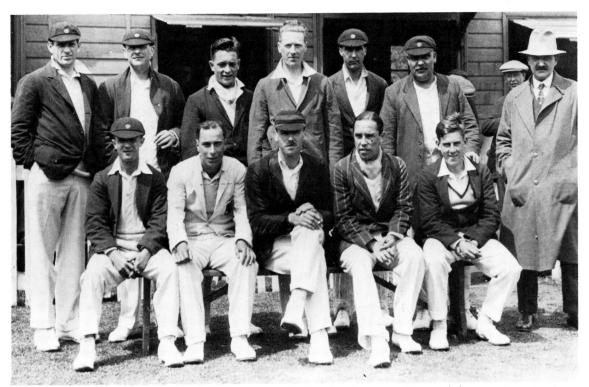

193. The County Cricket XI in the early Twenties, believed to be versus Warwickshire at Kettering in 1925. Note the difference between 'gentlemen' and 'players'. The 'players' (professionals) are wearing their county blazers and caps. The 'gentlemen' (amateurs) are with one exception capless. The team includes (*standing*) A. Thomas, a fast bowler (first left), C. N. Woolley (second left), A. H. Bull (third left) and (*sitting*) Fred 'Fanny' Walden (first on left), R. L. Wright (second left) and J. E. Timms (fifth from left). In the striped cap is J. M. Fitzroy, county captain 1924–7.

194. Miss Beatrice Cartwright presenting prizes at Brackley Show, 1927.

LANDOWNERS

195. Edwardian panache, Charles Robert,
the 6th Earl Spencer, who died in 1922.

196. Post-war pressures on the landowners: sales notice of part of the Knightley estates in 1932. Richard Knightley purchased Fawsley in 1416 and at its peak the Knightley estate in the County was just over 8,000 acres in extent. It was sold up in the Thirties, and the house at Fawsley abandoned.

197. New property owners: Lieutenant-Colonel Herbert Wareham Clinch, JP, of Blisworth House. Born at St. John's, New Brunswick, he served 30 years in the British army and saw action in the Boer War and the Great War. In 1920 he purchased Blisworth House at the great sale of the Duke of Grafton's Northamptonshire property. He broke his neck in a hunting accident in 1925.

198. Long-established landowners: the presentation of the Weldon quarrymen's gift of a silver salver to Viscount Maidstone on his coming of age in June 1933. On his left is his father, the Earl of Winchilsea, and on his right his mother, the Countess. The Finch-Hattons ceased to live in the County in the eighteenth century, letting Kirby Hall fall into ruin, but they retained their land and valuable quarrying and mineral rights.

199. Social duties: Lord Lilford in his masonic regalia as Provincial Grand Master for Northamptonshire and Huntingdonshire, Chairman at the 122nd Annual Festival of the Royal Masonic Institute for Boys in 1920. In that Festival in London some £88,000 was raised for this boys' school.

200. Social duties. The Duke of Gloucester opening the new premises of the Roadmender Youth Club in Northampton in 1936. Seen with him is Ernest Harrison, its founder. He called it 'Roadmender' because it was intended 'to steer its members through the danger spots in the road through adolescence'. *Roland Holloway.*

201. The opening of the new Nurses' Home at the General Hospital, Northampton, in 1938. From the left are the Marquess of Exeter, Earl Spencer, the Duchess of Gloucester, Mr. E. Bordoli, Alderman A. W. Lyne (the Mayor) and Lord Hesketh (standing), chairman of the Management Committee. *Roland Holloway.*

202. The wedding of George Brudenell-Bruce (later Brudenell), squire of Deene, and Miss Mary Schillizzi of Guilsborough in London in 1923. Mr. Brudenell died in 1962, and his wife 10 years later.

203. The 7th Earl Spencer in costume as one of his ancestors, Sir Robert Spencer,
1st Lord Spencer, with his wife as Queen Anne of Denmark, and their children
at an historical pageant at Althorp in 1932. The event was in aid of the local
Nursing Association. *Roland Holloway*.

204. The squire as musician: Gervase Elwes (1866–1921), Catholic squire of Billing, was one of the finest tenors of his day. Originally in the diplomatic service he became a professional singer and was noted for his musicianly interpretations of German lieder and English song. He was also much admired for his performances of Elgar's *Gerontius*. He was tragically killed in a train accident on tour in the USA.

206. Squire's daughter as historian. The daughter of Sir Herewald Wake of Courteenhall, Joan Wake became interested in historical research in her twenties, taught herself to read old handwriting and medieval Latin, and dedicated herself to research and the preservation of the local records of the past, then disappearing rapidly. In 1922 she founded the Northamptonshire Record Society, and is seen here collecting the ancient records of the Borough of Daventry by the sackful in 1935 for deposit at the County Record Office. Both these organizations are housed at Delapré Abbey in Northampton, an ancient house which she did so much to save when threatened with demolition after the Second World War.

205. Gyles Isham (1903–76) who succeeded to his father's baronetcy of Lamport in 1941, was a professional actor in the inter-war period. He achieved critical acclaim as an undergraduate *Hamlet* at Oxford in 1924, and went on to make a name in Shakespearian and other roles in London and Stratford-upon-Avon in the next fifteen years or so. He went to Hollywood and acted in the Greta Garbo film *Anna Karenina*. After war service he returned to Lamport to live the life of a scholarly country gentleman. He is seen here as Bolingbroke in a 1929 production of Shakespeare's *Richard II*.

207. A house party at Rushton Hall in August 1923. Rushton had been leased by Mr. L. Breitmeyer (right of centre in light suit and hat) who had made a fortune in diamonds in South Africa, and in 1923 his family decided to revive the old pre-war flower show. The guests included Major Cockayne Maunsell of Thorpe Malsor (behind Mr. Breitmeyer's right shoulder) and his wife (third from left). The clergyman on the right was the rector, Canon E. O. Jones. *Spencer Percival.*

208. Float at the Rushton Flower Festival 1923 depicting the Women's Land Army in the Great War.

209. Float at the same festival: Britannia and her allies in the Great War.

210. The Marchioness of Northampton (left) and
Mrs. Wentworth-Watson of Rockingham at a fête in aid of
the Women's Institute movement at Rushton Hall in 1923.
Spencer Percival.

ROYAL
OCCASIONS

211. The aura of royalty: Queen Mary on a visit to a
Brington garden fête in September 1937, during a
week's stay at Althorp. *Roland Holloway.*

212. The Prince of
Wales (later King
Edward VIII) at the
School for Girls,
St. George's Avenue,
Northampton, 7 July
1927. *Roland Holloway.*

213. The Prince of
Wales enjoys a joke
with the headmaster
(W. C. C. Cooke) and
the Mayor of
Northampton
(Councillor James
Peach) on a visit the
same day to the Town
and County School,
Northampton.
Roland Holloway.

214. Children of the Beckett and Sergeant Charity School in their traditional
uniforms await the Prince of Wales on the steps of All Saints Church,
Northampton, 7 July 1927.

215. The visit of the Duke and Duchess of York (later King George VI and Queen Elizabeth) to
Northampton in 1932 to open the new College of Technology and the John Greenwood Shipman home.
Whilst the other members of the official party are rather stiff and formal, the Duchess (the present Queen
Mother) is seen radiating the charm for which she is famous. With the royal couple are the Mayor and
Mayoress, Councillor and Mrs. P. F. Hanafy, Colonel John Brown and John Williamson, the
Chief Constable. *Roland Holloway.*

216. Royalty off duty: the Duke of York (later King George VI) out with the Pytchley in the mid-Twenties. He and his brothers were regular visitors to the County in the inter-war years and the Duke took houses for the hunting season at Guilsborough and Naseby at this time.

217. Formal wedding photograph of the Duke and Duchess of Gloucester, 3 September 1935. The Duke shortly afterwards purchased the Barnwell estate in Northamptonshire, the home of the present Duke. The bride was Lady Alice Montagu-Douglas-Scott, daughter of the Duke of Buccleuch. The present Queen is seated on the left and Princess Margaret on the right. *The Press Association.*

218. The residents of Compton Street, Northampton, celebrate the Jubilee of King George V and Queen Mary, 6 May 1935, with a street party.

219. The Drapery, Northampton, decorated for the Coronation of King George VI on 12 May 1937.

220. The start of the official celebrations to mark the Jubilee of King George V in Northampton, 6 May 1935. The Mayor (Alderman Burrows) is on the right of the mace, and on its left is the ex-Mayor, Councillor Allitt. On the extreme left is the Town Clerk (W. R. Kew) and on the extreme right is Chief Constable Williamson.

221. Workers in the factory of Long Buckby Shoes Ltd. sit down to a celebration tea to mark the Coronation of King George VI. Standing on the left are Mr. B. W. Cunnington (managing director) and Mrs. Cunnington.

INTER-WAR
POLITICS

222. Lord Birkenhead (F. E. Smith) (left) in Northampton
to support the election campaign of Captain A. F. G. Renton
(right) in May 1929. Lord Birkenhead, the foremost lawyer
of his day and a great political figure, had a country house
in the County, at Charlton. In the middle is
Mr. J. J. Martin. *Roland Holloway.*

223. C. A. McCurdy, Liberal MP for Northampton 1910–23. He was a strong supporter of the post-war coalition under Lloyd George and became Food Controller in that government in 1920.
W. Illingworth.

224. The emergence of the Labour Party. Margaret Bondfield, who had risen in the Labour movement as an organizer of women's trade unions, unsuccessfully opposed McCurdy in the elections of 1920 and 1922. In 1923, however, she defeated him, and although herself defeated at Northampton the following year, she went on to become the first woman to sit in the Cabinet.

226. Visit of Mr. and Mrs Winston Churchill to Northampton in April 1922 on behalf of the Coalition Government to support McCurdy. In front are seen (from the left) Mrs. McCurdy, Churchill, Mrs. Churchill and Sir James Crockett, a prominent local Liberal and shoe manufacturer. Behind them are (from the left) Sir Ryland Adkins, Liberal MP for Middleton and Prestwich, Captain A. E. Fitzroy, Unionist MP for Daventry (and later Speaker of the House of Commons), Mr. A. E. Marlow, another prominent local shoe manufacturer, the Hon. Mrs. A. E. Fitzroy, Major H. L. C. Brassey, Unionist MP for the Peterborough Division, and C. A. McCurdy.

225. *Left* The twilight of Northampton Liberalism. The visit of Mrs. Lloyd George, the Prime Minister's wife, in July 1921, to support McCurdy, against whom part of the local Liberal Party had turned. *Standing* (left to right) are McCurdy, Miss Bird, the Mayor of Northampton (W. Harvey Reeves), the ex-Mayor (F. Kilby), Mrs. Kilby, Sir Henry Randall, Mrs. Winterbottom and A. E. Marlow. *Sitting* (left to right) are the Mayoress (Mrs. Reeves), Mrs. Lloyd George, Mrs. Marlow, Miss Bouverie, Mrs. McCurdy and Lady Randall.

227. Electioneering in the Twenties.
Captain Renton in Northampton in 1929.

228. Electioneering in the Twenties. S. F. Perry in the 1929 election campaign. He was elected at Kettering in 1923 but had been defeated by Sir Mervyn Manningham-Buller in 1924. However, he was returned in 1929, only to lose his seat in the great Labour collapse of 1931. He was the father of Fred Perry, the tennis player. The *Daily Herald* in the Twenties was the chief voice of the Labour movement in Fleet Street and had a circulation of nearly 300,000. *Spencer Percival.*

229. *Overleaf* Declaration of the poll at Northampton 1928. Colonel C. J. L. Malone, the second Labour Member to sit for Northampton, had just defeated Captain Renton. The election was occasioned by the death of Sir A. E. A. Holland (Conservative) who had been MP since 1924. This was the first election in which the 'flappers' (women below the age of thirty) voted, but it was the intervention of an Independent Conservative which tipped the scales in favour of Malone. In the General Election of 1929 he again defeated Captain Renton.

231. Sir Mervyn Manningham-Buller, Conservative MP for Northampton 1931–40, with his wife and daughter at their Carlton home in 1935. An army officer, he had contested Heywood (Lancs.) in 1906 and 1910 and did not re-enter politics until 1924 (when he was 59). He represented Kettering 1924–29.

230. Colonel Cecil L'Estrange Malone, Labour MP for Northampton 1928–31.

232. A Conservative political meeting believed to be in 1930, the speaker being
(it is thought) Sir Arthur de Capell Brooke. The lavish use of the Union flag on
the platform is a reminder that it was at this time that the Conservatives
developed the line that they were the party of 'all the people', a theme which has
remained central in their publicity ever since. At this time women
Conservatives organized 'Union Jack bazaars', and this photograph seems to have
been taken at one. *Spencer Percival.*

233. Declaration of the poll at Northampton in 1935. The Labour candidate,
R. T. Paget, addresses the crowd after his defeat by Sir Mervyn Manningham-
Buller. Paget then nursed the Northampton seat for 10 years, being returned in the
great Labour victory of 1945. He held the seat until his retirement in 1974 – a
remarkable achievement. *Roland Holloway.*

THE APPROACH
OF WAR

234. Territorial Army recruiting poster probably dating from
March 1939 when the Secretary of State for War doubled the
strength of the Territorial Battalions. By then the old
4th Battalion of the Northamptons had become Gunners
and a new 4th Battalion was being raised.

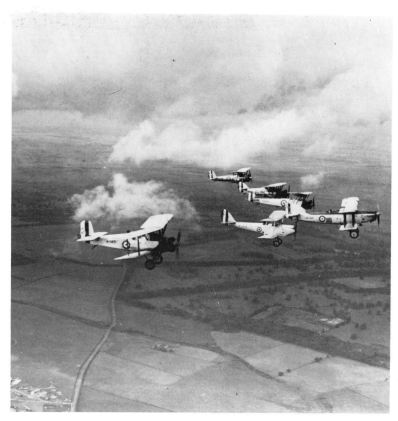

235. Formation of various types of aircraft used by the Central Flying School over Wittering airfield. Wittering had been re-opened in 1926 as the Central Flying School for the Royal Air Force. It became the Flying Training School in 1935 and an operational fighter base in 1938. *Flight International.*

236. Lynx Avro of the Central Flying School demonstrating a blind take-off in the early Thirties. *Flight International.*

237. Signallers of the Northamptonshire Regiment practising semaphore at Gibraltar Barracks, Northampton, just after war had been declared in late 1939.
Roland Holloway.

238. A weapons training cadre of corporals of the Northamptons with the new two-inch mortar at Northampton Barracks in 1939. The instructors are Sgt. Ariss (left) and Sgt. Ward.
Roland Holloway.

239. Waiting for the Luftwaffe: two regulars at the
Gibraltar Barracks with the new Bren Gun of 1939. It was
(optimistically) for use against low-flying aircraft as well
as infantry. *Roland Holloway.*